It was Christmas Day. I was on honeymoon. In Jerusalem. Well, where would *you* go for your day trip?

So I woke up, bright-eyed and bushy-tailed, and announced to my wife of five days:

"Happy Christmas! We're going to Bethlehem!"

Bethlehem was only seven miles from our Jerusalem guesthouse. Lucy and I would get to stand there and imagine a pregnant woman and her husband arriving 2,000 years ago, right there in those streets, looking for somewhere to stay as the labour pains started.

We'd get to look at the fields and imagine the shepherds out there with their sheep, in those very fields.

It would be marvellous. What could go wrong?

Here's what went wrong.

I had forgotten that there was a wall in the way.

I hadn't really thought through the politics of the Middle East as I organised the trip or made our Christmas Day plans. With everything else that was going on with the wedding and honeymoon arrangements, I'd forgotten that there's a wall between Jerusalem and Bethlehem, between Israel and the West Bank. Built in 2003, it is in most places at least 8 metres high. It stretches for 485 miles. And it is a major obstacle if you are trying to get from Jerusalem to Bethlehem with your bride on Christmas Day.

We queued for hours. Guards with guns patrolled the lines. Happy Christmas!

I think you could say it sucked the romance out of the day a bit.

THIS IS WHY IT MATTERS

I don't know if you've ever spent Christmas in a strange place. That's certainly the weirdest location for Christmas morning I've ever ended up in—standing at the place that perhaps best sums up one of this world's most insurmountable divisions.

Right now, as you read this booklet, there's still a wall between Jerusalem and Bethlehem. And right now, there are walls between couples, between siblings, between parents and children—walls running through lounges as families gather (or don't gather) for Christmas. Maybe you're all too painfully aware of the relational wall separating members of your family. That's the reality. We cover it with tinsel, turkey and TV. But even at Christmas—sometimes, especially at Christmas—this is a world of walls.

Jesus—God's own Son—left heaven to come into this world.

He was born in an animal shelter in Bethlehem because a Roman emperor whose armies were occupying Israel decided to send everyone back to their home towns for a census.

His parents would have shared the road from Nazareth to Bethlehem with occupying soldiers.

He was born into a reality not so different from the reality of today's world.

So this booklet isn't going to tell the story of Christmas. Most of us have appeared in (and, if you're a parent, sat through) enough Nativity plays to know the outline of the story: Mary, Gabriel, pregnancy, Bethlehem, baby Jesus, manger, shepherds, angels, wise men, gold, frankincense and myrrh.

That's the story of Christmas—but I want to focus on the *significance* of Christmas—which, ironically, becomes easier and easier to miss the more and more familiar the story sounds to us.

And, standing there at that wall, I realised: This, *right here,* is why Christmas matters. At the first Christmas, Jesus was born to join us on this earth not because everything here is great and he wanted to join the party. No—he came because things are not as they should be in this world of walls.

THE REASON FOR THE WALLS

The first Christmas was an utterly supernatural event. It involved angels—who, by the way, are powerful spiritual beings who act as God's messengers, rather than small girls dressed in a white sheet with a tinsel-based headband. And when God sent an angel to

Mary's fiancé, Joseph, to tell him what was about to happen, the angel told him:

> *"[Mary] will give birth to a son, and you are to give him the name Jesus, because he will save his people from their sins." (The Gospel of Matthew, chapter 1, verse 21)*

That message diagnosed the reason for the walls in our world. The word "sins" sums up what's gone wrong. Sins are not just doing things that are a bit wrong, or even very wrong. Sins are the actions and attitudes that spring from a decision to reject the loving authority of the God who made all things. That's the sin that lies beneath all sins. It's the choice to live without a relationship with our Maker—to say to him, "This is my life, and I will live by my rules". Sin is taking all that God gives—life, breath, friendship, love, fun—and ignore, or abuse, the Giver.

It's the choice to live, as the Bible puts it, "alienated from God and ... enemies in your mind" (Colossians 1 v 21). Though we don't tend to think of it this way, we choose conflict—war—with the God who made us and gives us everything we have.

Right now, there is a wall in each of our hearts. It's a wall we build to keep God out—to keep him off the throne of our lives, so that we can carry on saying, in effect, "My life, my rules".

And that's what builds all the other walls. The Bible says that, from the very first rejection of God back in the mists of human history, turning our backs on God means turning our backs on each other. John Stuart Mill, one of the fathers of modern liberalism and economic theory, was on to something when he wrote back in the nineteenth century:

"We are self-seeking individuals looking to maximise the optimum benefit for ourselves from every decision."

This is what we're like. Putting ourselves rather than God at the centre of our lives—looking to maximise the optimum benefit for ourselves—damages our relationships with humanity. Sin constructs a wall between ourselves and our God—and between ourselves and each other. It runs between peoples, along borders; and it runs between people, within workplaces and families and homes.

I didn't grow up in a Christian home, but as a teenager I realised that something was badly wrong, both with me and with the world. It actually came as quite a relief to discover what the problem was: the truth that I sin, because humanity sins.

And I remember being struck by this truth on honeymoon that Christmas Day as we waited at the wall.

I mentioned it to Lucy. It didn't improve the romantic atmosphere very much.

WAR IS OVER (EXCEPT IT ISN'T)

The wall in our own hearts explains why we can't tear down the walls in our own lives and throughout our world. It explains why we just don't seem able to stop the wars, end all poverty and guarantee justice.

Over 45 years ago, John Lennon wished us a "Happy Xmas" and promised us that "War Is Over (If You Want It)". Well, more than 45 Christmases have passed, and the wars have never stopped, however much we all want them to.

WHY?

When we reject relationship with God and reject the good, wise rule of God in our lives, it damages our relationships. You don't need me to tell you how that looks on a personal level—so many of us know the pain, the regret and the sadness all too well. And on a geopolitical level, it looks like walls between people—be it Hadrian's Wall, the Berlin Wall, or the one between Jerusalem and Bethlehem.

Truth is, it's no better in the world of religion, either. Maybe that's what puts you off church. There's a photograph that sums up the religious walls that our sin can build—a photo of two churches, in an English town, right next to each other. In the middle of the 1800s, there was such an angry falling out in the congregation of St Mary's in Stoke Newington that half of them went directly next door and built their own church. So there are these two churches, right next to one another, and they stand as a reminder of the way humanity is so very good at allowing division and causing conflict, and so very bad at ending disputes and finding peace.

Happy Christmas!

But keep reading—keep listening to the message of the angel. We've seen how he summed up the *problem* in one word—sins. He also described the *solution* in another single word…

SAVE

> *"He will save his people from their sins."*

Christmas is not about us having a happy day while ignoring the problem; it is about God getting involved in human history to solve the problem. (And when you grasp that, Christmas Day becomes truly happy.)

At the first Christmas, God's Son became a man. Jesus lived a perfect life. Jesus never rejected his Father, our Creator. Yet at the other end of his earthly life from lying in the manger, Jesus died hanging on a cross. And he did that in order to experience the misery of complete separation from his Father that we have chosen by rejecting relationship with him. He died to bring us forgiveness so that we could enjoy coming into friendship with God—not just in this life, but for ever. Jesus came to save people from the consequences of their sin. He came to break down the walls we build between ourselves and our God. He came to announce that, in the most cosmic, most eternal, and most significant sense:

> *"War Is Over (If You Want It)."*

Happy Christmas!

And once the wall between us and God is broken down by his forgiveness of us, and we're at peace with our Creator, we can start to break down the other walls with the same dynamite—the dynamite of forgiveness.

HOW TO ENJOY PEACE

There are two great things about being a pastor at Christmastime. The first is that you get lots of presents, including some hilarious ones. One year, someone gave me a bright pink jumper. Another, someone gave me a dog bowl. (I don't have a dog.)

The second is that you get to choose what you talk about at carol services and no one can stop you. So last year, I picked a Bible verse that sounds as if it has nothing to do with Christmas. I chose it because I think that in fact it has *everything* to do with Christmas. It's this:

> *"Bear with each other and forgive one another if any of you has a grievance against someone. Forgive as the Lord forgave you." (Colossians 3 v 13)*

If you want to experience peace this Christmas... if there's a wall between you and someone else and you would love it to come down... you need to grasp this verse.

Christmas is a time of great joy and also of great reflection. It's a time when the good things in life are seen clearest, but also when the walls and the regrets and the mistakes and unfulfilled hopes loom largest. So many of us can't wait for Christmas, but others of us can't wait to get through it. Most of us enjoy it and yet, at the same time, we have a tinge of sadness about some element of it—and often that sadness is caused by the knowledge that, to some extent and in one way or another, we've put up walls.

Maybe it's a wall between a married couple who've stopped really talking to one another or listening to one another. Each is waiting for the other partner to change—then they'll dismantle the wall (maybe).

Maybe it's a wall between a parent and a child, where both feel let down or not listened to or unappreciated or unloved by the other.

Maybe it's a wall between two old friends, where a forgotten birthday or a lack of phone calls or a shortage of sympathy at some point has seen everything go cold.

How can we change? How can this Christmas really be one of peace and love and joy?

Only if it's a Christmas of forgiveness. And you get the power to forgive, and to ask others to forgive you, by seeing what God was doing the first Christmas, in the coming of Jesus.

> *"Forgive as the Lord forgave you."*

So here are the three steps to taking down the walls.

1. You realise that actually Jesus really was born in Bethlehem. Christianity has historical clothes. It's not based on a philosophy or a mantra or a feeling. It's based on historical events. It happened in Bethlehem, in the town I finally stood in, after the hours of queuing at the wall that Christmas Day. It happened, as the carol puts it, "once in royal David's city". Jesus really walked the roads of Israel, just as I did on honeymoon. He really did die on a cross—and, yes, he really did rise again from death.

   And of course, this may be more than you're willing to accept right now, because as you think about it you find it very hard to believe. Well, that's good—what matters is to think about it, and to look into the evidence for these events. Please do! It may be stronger than you've been thinking. But for the moment, please read on—because seeing what effect it would have if this were all true will motivate you to find out if it really is true.

2. You realise the meaning of what happened in history—that Jesus came to help you, to save you and to change you. You understand that he was born because he loves you and that he died because he wants to forgive you.

3. You accept what you are being offered—forgiveness from God and friendship with God. You say,

   > *"Yes, God, this is for me. This is what Christmas, and life, is going to be all about. I want to say to you, 'My life, your rules'. I want to admit my sin, and to accept and enjoy your forgiveness. I want to be at peace with you, rather than at war with you."*

   And so you walk through life knowing that the most important wall has come down; and that the most important Person in the universe loves you. You're forgiven by the Lord, and now you're in a position to begin to "forgive as the Lord forgave you". C.S. Lewis, who became a Christian in his thirties and went on to write the Narnia books, put it like this:

   > *"To be Christian means to forgive the indefensible in other people because God has forgiven the indefensible in you."*

   In many ways, true Christianity looks like forgiveness.

STILL WITH US

Jesus doesn't only call us to forgive, or even merely show us how to forgive—he empowers his friends to forgive.

At the first Christmas, Jesus was given a nickname:

"'The virgin will conceive and give birth to a son, and they will call him Immanuel' (which means 'God with us')." (Matthew 1 v 23)

"God with us"—that's the nickname. As we look in that manger in history, we can say, *There was God— Immanuel—come to be with people.* But it's even better than that, because Jesus can be with us today. At the other end of his time on earth, after he'd risen and before he returned to rule in heaven, Jesus promised his friends:

"Surely I am with you always, to the very end of the age."
(Matthew 28 v 20)

The God who lived on earth 2,000 years ago now lives with his people through his Spirit. C.S. Lewis did not forgive others through his own efforts. He forgave because he had God with him: the Spirit changing him. If you know you need to forgive, or ask for forgiveness… if you know you need to give up that anger, stop replaying that wrong, cease plotting your revenge… if you know a wall needs taking down… you need to look *back* at God's Son, and see that he came to be with you and forgive you. You need to accept his offer of friendship. And then you need to look *in* at God's Spirit coming to be with you and empower you.

The Bible makes clear that the Christian faith is not just about believing in a Creator God who is way up there. It's not just about looking back to the figure of Jesus, who lived centuries ago, way back then. The essence of life as a Christian is not God's distance from us, but God's presence with us, by his Spirit, so we can enjoy his forgiveness and reach out to others in forgiveness.

The 18th-century English poet Alexander Pope wrote, "To err is human; to forgive, divine". God knows that, and so he sends his Spirit to strengthen us, to melt our hearts, and to enable us to say two phrases that will be at the heart of any truly peace-filled Christmas. Here they are:

"I'm sorry, I was wrong—please forgive me."

"That's OK. I forgive you."

It may take time. It may take patience. It may even be that the door keeps being slammed in your face despite your request for or offer of forgiveness. (And if that happens, then at least you'll be able to appreciate a little more how God's Son, having come at the first Christmas, felt to be greeted, in large part, by indifference and opposition.) But these are the first steps. These are the basis of a truly peace-filled Christmas. And you'll only find the motivation to forgive others, and to ask for forgiveness from others, as you ask for and find forgiveness from God—in other words, you will "forgive" as you appreciate how "the Lord forgave you."

PEACE ON EARTH

The angels were busy at the first Christmas. After Jesus had been born, a whole choir's-worth of angels appeared in those fields outside Bethlehem. And here's what they said:

> *"Glory to God in the highest heaven, and on earth peace to those on whom his favour rests." (Luke 2 v 14)*

"On earth peace." This is Christmas—the message of the first Christmas and the reason for the first Christmas. War is over,